CONTENTS

REMEMBERING DAME MYRA HESS

Most beautiful, most gifted, and most wise,
How shall man word the wonder that you were,
Now that your grace no longer blesses eyes,
Your presence nulls no care?
You are set free, as music that you played,
Made life a glory as your fingers bade,
You are alive with all that never dies.

For surely now you are among the rays
That guide and bless our darkness, as we grope
From wreck to ruin in life's tangled maze,
Lighting the paths of Hope . . .
Wisdom that sent you still directs your giving
The Courage that determines all things living
To seek for beauty and to light the ways.

I see you, as upon your stage alone,
In the great breathless silence that awaits
You, with the touches that make beauty known
Unbarring the shut gates . . .
You, the clear-eyed, who saw, in the attempt,
Eternal sparks illumine the dream dreamt,
The starry hand that scattered the seed sown.

FOR LUKE O'CONNOR

One early Summer, when the times were bad,
In 'Little Old New York', long years ago,
I looked for work, an ignorant raw lad,
Knowing no craft, nor knowing how to know.

There, up and down, in the exciting Sun,
I offered help that no one seemed to need,
Then suddenly success came; Life had won;
Luke offered work, and I was saved indeed.

Saved and restarted, with the golden chance
(At last) of learning what mankind has wrought
In all his centuries of ignorance;
To light his darkness with the stars of thought.

These are belated thanks, but let me say,
'For seventy years I've thanked you every day.'

THE CURLEWS

We three were in wild Shropshire, picking sloes,
Shropshire where Wrekin stands and Severn flows,
Fortune had set glad feathers in our caps,
After fierce storms, hot tropics and ill-haps.
And who can tell aright the joy we felt
There, in that happy chance by Fortune dealt?

In the red west, the sun was sinking low,
With baskets full of sloes we turned to go,
But paused, to watch the light on waste and pond
Put colour on the hills in Wales beyond,
And heard the church bells tell the time afar
Above dim graves wherein our kinsmen are.

And looking at that Shropshire scene I cried,
'No sunset sees a lovelier country-side:
This waste of sloes; the cornfield with its stooks,
The last sun on the elms, with the last rooks,
What would improve such beauty; nay, what could?'
My great friend said, 'Some birds might . . . curlews would.'

And at her word a cry of curlews came,
Crying their cry of creatures never tame,
That marvellous cry that birds make out of breath
Whose marvellous meaning we may know at death.
This, like her lovely spirit, made us know,
All the scene's soul, that had been only show.

A SONG OF WAKING

The stars are dim before the Sun has risen;
The sky they stell is as a windless lake
That seems to need a word, that seems to listen
For unheard order bidding morning break.
The word for the unlocking of the prison,
To bid the Sun arise and men awake.

Awake; the peacocks roosting on the boughs
Scream, and fly down, with scatterings of dew;
Up, in their cote the tumbler pigeons rouse,
A distant cock crows, and is answered-to.
The world is all awaking from its drowse,
To the day's trouble and the work to do.

Within the Tower, ringers' fingers grope
By lantern-light, and, at a word, their heaves,
Jangling awhile, bring music from the rope,
Startling the jackdaws nesting in the eaves.
The jangling stumbles into tune with Hope,
'Awake, and try, even if Death bereaves.'

Awake, for from the never-pastured whins,
The morning brings the light of a new day.
The Night is gone, the Morning re-begins,
Up, man, awake and ask what people say:
'Was there no room in any of the inns,
For other strangers who might show the way?'

Away, all pilgrims, to your pilgrimage,
Though the Sun shine not, you have still the light,
The Day unfolds, a fair, unwritten page,
Awakened hearts will tell you what to write,
And you the specks upon a starry stage
Have still a Day before the unknown Night.

Away, awake, before the day is old,
Somewhere, in every heart it's April still,
April with little lambkins out of fold,
The black-thorn and the yellow daffodil,
In mud by happy brooks, the marigold,
And married blackbird cocks with golden bill.

THE SHROPSHIRE FRIENDS

Long since, when coming from the West,
With England near, I could not rest,
Though night time fell,
So near the two that I loved best.

There, somewhere, nor-nor-east from me,
Was Shropshire, where I longed to be,
Ercall and Mynd,
Severn and Wrekin, you and me.

So up I went, to walk the deck,
To gaze, with eager aching neck,
For England's Lights,
The Lighthouses preventing wrecks.

Far forward I would crane, to spy
Those fixed stars of the sailor's eye,
His most loved stars,
And feel their beauty drawing nigh.

There, while the beating engines shed
The mumble of their trampled tread,
The ship's great heart,
I stared into the night ahead.

Into a darkness now I stare
Towards where Wrekin lifts in air
And Severn glides,
I know that you are somewhere there.

WHAT THE WREKIN GAVE

You matchless two, to whom I owe
That comradeship of long ago,
Those times past praise,
That Sun, when all life else was snow,
You gladden all an old man's woe,
With joy that glows and stays.

THE HILL

I see yon harebells, foxgloves, brooks,
All glistening from rain,
The cruising kestrels and the rooks
And haunted hill again.

Haunted with something from of old
That lays a ghostly hand . . .
There being spirit in the mould
Men cannot understand.

O hill of wonder and delight,
Of joy too deep for tears
Day splendour, steadfast in the night,
And comrade through the years.

O miracle of earthly joy
Since before life began,
Who comforted a broken boy,
And staunched a broken man.

Take what of blessing age can give
O marvel vast and dumb,
And O, be with me while I live
And mine through what's to come.

THE MERRY SWEVVY

O water rushing through the grass,
In England's ancient times,
A poet slumbered where you pass
And dreamed of England's crimes.

O water babbling as you take
Your freedom down the slopes,
Babble to me, till I awake
And sing of England's hopes.

CAER OCVRAN

There are some ramparts in the distant West,
A heave of hill, once castled for a king,
But now a sheep-walk where the curlews nest,
And wild bees hive, and many skylarks sing.

Once, a heart beat here in a Queen of fable,
Child of a King here, still in people's tales,
Beat in a pulse that made her crown unstable,
But pardoned now, where beauty still avails.

Now, where she lived and rode, the curlews call
Their marvellous cry, that opens doors unseen,
Into a world wherein no sinners fall,
But Destiny sets crowns on King and Queen.

And though the realm fell and the hearts were riven
The heart that beat to beauty is forgiven.

I DREAMED

'I dreamed a dream the other night . . .
Lowlands, lowlands, hurray, my John'

I dreamed, that all that poets wrote was true,
Or had been true, and known as true, of old,
When skies, that shone on Helen, were more blue
And crowns, on such as Priam, were more gold.

That still, if Fortune favoured, I might find
One who had seen the Muses in their dance,
And, for his seeing, had been stricken blind,
But blest, till death, his paradisal chance.

That, in some glen, of always blossomed thorn,
I, keeping in its shadow, still might see,
White, like the moon at full, the Unicorn,
Licking the granites where the crystals be.

That still, I might perceive, within her pyre
Of burning spikenard, her Arabian coal,
The Phoenix' self all beautiful with fire
Singing a new song that would shake the soul.

That, still, I might hear Niobe make moan,
Imploring speech from beauty without breath,
Where her too lovely children, turned to stone,
Stand, or lie silent, in their place of death.

That, still, elsewhere, on wings, the sacred Child
Returned to life, would come out of the sea
With brightness purifying the defiled,
Illumining, restoring setting free . . .

He, with his ship of souls, bound to the West,
With all her crew of glory singing hymns,
To say that dying shall be dispossest
And life return where the sky never dims.

A FELLOW MORTAL

I found a fox, caught by the leg
In a toothed gin, torn from its peg,
And dragged, God knows how far, in pain.

Such torment could not plead in vain,
He looked at me, I looked at him.
With iron jaw-teeth in his limb.

'Come, little son,' I said, 'Let be . . .
Don't bite me, while I set you free.'

But much I feared that in the pang
Of helping, I should feel a fang
In hand or face . . .
                        but must is must . . .
And he had given me his trust.

So down I knelt there in the mud
And loosed those jaws all mud and blood.
And he, exhausted, crept, set free,
Into the shade, away from me;

The leg not broken . . .
                        Then, beyond,
That gin went plonk into the pond.

THE THROCKMORTON COAT

John Coxeter, who owned the Greenham Mill,
Employed a hundred hands, and praised their skill.
And being challenged, said, 'Let facts decide . . .
The hands are here: the matter shall be tried.
I undertake that fleeces shall be shorn.
Made yarn, made cloth, made as a coat and worn
Within the compass of a Summer's day.'

When that year's cuckoos could not rightly say
Their own known name, the feat had been prepared,
The artists picked, the lesser workings shared,
All England talked of what she was to see,
And much of England said it could not be . . .
But growled that 'these machines had gone too far,
These boasting men would surely have a jar
And fail in their attempt, and rightly fail.'

Fine summer weather was on Kennet Vale.
The corn-crake called; the nightjar churred and clocked,
And towards Newbury the thousands flocked.

There on the morrow, Greenham folk would try
To show a skill to be remembered by,
They did not doubt, but doubters were at hand,
To say how chance might ruin the deed planned.
'We know the Greenham skill, and all it means,
But who trusts skill depending on machines?
A summer's day is but a summer's day,
And every process tried may bring delay.
We feel, in short, that boasters cannot thrive
And, too, what madness to begin at Five,
Throwing away an hour, starting late.'

14

The summer night brought on the day of Fate,
All Newbury was up, and crowds arriving
Thronged towards Greenham to behold the striving,
And as the clocks struck Five, the umpires cried,
'The contest has begun: let right decide.'
And instantly a shepherd brought to view
Two Southdown sheep and promptly sheared the two,
With the swift skill, so marvellously sure
Their victims ever trust them and endure.

The shearing took some time: the wool, when shorn,
Looked much unlike a garment to be worn,
That greasy heap of sheep's wool, fouled and rough
No coat as yet, though possibly the stuff.

The doubters, ever wise, were heard to say,
'No coat from that will see this summer's day . . .
They started late, and having just begun,
Of fifteen processes have finished one.
We'll to the side shows for delight is there
With all the wonders of a country fair.'

I, as a boy, worked in a weaving mill
Whose clanging looms have been a long while still,
And there, in the noon-breaks, we would tell over
What processes we knew, or could discover
Between the shorn fleece and the woven thing,
Some thirty odd, in all our numbering,
But half of these belonged to our own age
Eighty years later than the Berkshire stage.

Still, let us reckon that the Berkshire men
Had fifteen processes before them then
With one now done, and fourteen still to do.

The day's task seems divided into two.
One, to make cloth from wool, and one to fit
The task's supporter in a coat of it.
One who believed that Britons brought to bay,
Will stand as one and show the world the way.

A friend to Greenham there; a man to note,
Who gave his name to the Throckmorton Coat,
Then but a frowzy heap upon the floor,
With one thing done demanding fourteen more.

The next task was to pick the fleeces clear
Of thorns and tangles gathered in the year,
Then, to make yarn of them, their tooth-combs plied:
The wool was softened, smoothed and scarified,
Into a softness like a summer mist
Untwisted and then spun to other twist,
Made into yarn, then loomed; and then began
Triumphant skill, a master weaving man,
Coxeter's young son, famous in the art,
Of weaving, wove, and played a master's part,
He at his loom created the new thing
Cloth from the yarn, like April from the Spring,
The Kersey showed, in spite of checks and snaps
And stoppages, delayings and mishaps
The woven fabric showed, and watchers cheered.
But let none think that sudden triumph neared,
The web grew slowly, slowly, though it grew,
And other processes were still to do,
And though the loom was slow, the hours flew.

Meanwhile, all Newbury made holiday,
In many an old and now forgotten way.
There, on an open stage, the Back-Sword men

Old Berkshire Gamesters, very famous then
Challenged the youth from every Berkshire town,
To come and take a knock or win a crown
'For glory, or a new hat, or for both.'
(The young men took the challenge, nothing loth.)

Mummers and tumblers played where the crowds swarmed
In quiet corners conjurors performed.
Where dogs were not allowed, the dancing bears
Shuffled slow side-steps to men's whistled airs,
And high above all other noises rose
The pan pipes of the Punch and Judy shows,
With shouts of 'Rollo Bowl-O' in a rally
Of well aimed whackets flung at Old Aunt Sally.

All of the sports of any country fair
Were ranked indeed to win men's pennies there.
The summer sun was bright in the blue sky
And one by one the Greenham tasks went by.
Until a change came and the feeling heightened
And many a face, that had been betting, whitened
For now the tug drew near, and long delay
Checked, as a snowdrift fallen on a way
Might check the Mails bringing a longed for news.

Between the Life and Death, or Win and Lose
Lies but a breath, and which way will it tend?

The weaving of the cloth had reached its end.
The fleeces were now cloth to public view,
Much had been done, but more remained to do,
The cloth must still be pressed, and trimmed, and dyed,
Then turned about in hot air till it dried . . .
Then, the dried Kersey, beautiful and bright,

With blue-bell blue, enchanting to the sight,
Had to be cut to measure, pieced and sewn,
Into the tailors' smartest fashion known.
Buttoned, where needed, button-holed where due,
And lined with silks, the finest London knew,
And, though delays might check, the summer sun
Riding the sky would be delayed by none.
The Time would pass . . .
                                    So many a sorry sigh
Wrung the hearts waiting for the web to dry.

At last, the web was dry and could be pieced
To needed measures . . .
                                    now, all babble ceased
Now, as in racers entering the Straight
The Greenham venturers drew sword with Fate.
For Four o'clock had struck, and now the Curtain
Trembled to fall to make the matter certain.

Twelve tailors waited, while a master hand
Cut the new cloth to measures subtly planned.
Each of the twelve received his piece to sew,
All happiness in life seemed long ago
To all the watchers in that Berkshire town
Could all be done before the sun went down?

Five struck, then Six . . .
                                    but now the ending neared,
The sewings finished and the room was cleared.
The Coat was fitted and was found to fit . . .
(Some small adjustments made perfected it.)
At twenty minutes after Six, a gun,
And bells, and cheers, declared that Greenham won,
An easy win, for, after starting late,

18

That summer sunset time was after Eight
The Greenham men had won by three good hours.

That June, with all her flowers,
The dog-rose in the hedge,
The King cup in the sedge,
The clover-cop most blest,
That saw the partridge nest,
Has passed, as all Junes must,
For Change has many powers.

But mortal men, who trust
That Effort brightens Dust,
May make the better best
And all the wonder ours.

THE STARS THAT SHONE

Now that I cannot get about
And know what I must do without,
I think of men of long ago
Whom I was privileged to know,
The men, like stars, showing the way.
They were Life's masterpieces; they . . .

Most, now, for many years have lain
Out in the churchyards in the rain,
In villages where clocks are slow.
And some where men no longer go
Now that a peace has been declared,
And times have changed since many cared.

Musicians, painters, poets, men
Who made the world more lovely then,
The story-tellers beyond price,
Bringing the news from Paradise,
Men from whose handiwork we see
Horizons in eternity.

Now that my roving days are over,
And all my frontiers stop at Dover,
I think of what Life used to mean
When all these fellows trod the scene
And Life was in myself with them
In Troy, in Greece, and Bethlehem.

Rich was the Life they let me share
Those spirits of the days that were.
Those dippers in the wells of art,
That found such cures for broken heart.

And such variety of friend
From Broken Heart to the World's End.

Their portraits still display the men . . .
Who, now, can match with those of then?
Those men who tamed the unbacked beasts,
And spoke the witty word at feasts,
And made the wicked world go round
Twixt Chance's Pitch and Lobs's Pound?

Some knew the seas whose Westers toss
The mollyhawk and albatross,
Whose mates the yellow fever killed
For graves that yellow fever filled.
Destroying strength, annulling youth,
From Benin Bight to Vera Cruz.

But all are gone, for the world turns,
And Change is what all living earns,
Change, and the Hope, that we may meet
Such lovely friends in a new street,
And share their never-ending joy
In Bethlehem, and Greece, and Troy.

TWO COUSINS
PART ONE
I

The delays in the Voyages' early months
Exploring Florida

John Hawkins, Cousin born to Francis Drake,
He, about thirty-four, Drake, twenty-three,
Had a small squadron, with command to take
The six ships south where golden pickings be.
He, in the Flag-ship of his little band,
Drake, in a small bark, in his first command.

The Africans proved war-like and unkind,
And weeks were passed as they collected slaves.
Four hundred living blacks whom they designed
To sell for gold across the western waves.
Three weeks should bring them to the west, but Fate
Again was harsh; the passage took them eight.

And worse than this, by strict new Spanish law
All traffic with the English was forbidden.
And all their promised harvest seemed but straw
And all attempt to trade had to be hidden.
But, still, many were sold, though plenty died,
And summer passed that never can abide.

They had to turn for home ere August ceased
For they had stayed too long in the great sun
When hurricanes and furies are released
And lightnings blind men's eyes, and thunders stun
All sailormen avoid and with good reason
The Spanish Main seas in the cyclone season.

But, off the Cuban Coast, a cyclone took them,
And broke the Flagship's rudder and took toll
Of all the squadron's garnishings and shook them;
And where were any docks to make them whole?
And here, perhaps, the cousins disagreed,
Each, being what he was, this was decreed.

To Hawkins, in command, in a Queen's ship,
And Florida at hand, all little known,
The chance suggested an exploring trip,
To find some haven for his squadron's own,
A bay with depth, and springs, safe for careening,
With wood to burn, while fitting out and cleaning.

To Drake, a seaman, English-Channel-bred,
Such havens were in plenty, north and west,
On the way home, fair islands without dread
Of Spanish cruisers coming to molest.
At all costs, they should turn to such as these,
Away from tempests in these Spanish seas.

Thus, as a Cousin, he could frankly urge,
But as a junior Captain earn, retort
They were in danger, but on safety's verge,
Within a four days' sail of such a port,
But Florida . . . why wander from one's way,
To wreck upon a shoal in Dead Man's Bay?

Hawkins, as Commodore, bade his fleet turn
To explore Florida, to find a nest
Fit for careening shipping, and to learn,
The unknown landscape stretching north and west.

They sailed a fortnight, sounding shoals and leaking
But found no shelter, such as they were seeking.

By this, they were well west, and the wind failed
And food and water failed, or were fast failing,
And Spaniards claimed the waters that they sailed,
And slaves were dying and the seamen ailing . . .
Now it was mid September, yet, how face
Atlantic autumn in their sorry case?

II
In the Gulf of Mexico
The decision to go to St John

What could be done to save them was debated.
Their ships needed refitting there and then.
(The Flagship needed to be recreated,)
Only a harbour lacked: they had the men.
The thousand miles of Gulf they wandered on
Had but one port, the harbour of St John.

This was their only hope, and this, alas,
In late September, would be held in force,
But all agreed, no other harbour was.
Towards this shelter Hawkins altered course.
As Cousin, not as seaman, doubtless Drake
Called such decision madness not mistake.

Did not the Cousin speak from a full heart:
'Sir, be advised; turn north and east for home,
Go where we have some knowledge or a chart,
St John is death: leave it to Spain and Rome.

24

By this time, Sir, the Spanish fleet is there,
With thousands more, for the September Fair.

'If, as I judge, the Spanish Fleet has come,
It will be there, with twenty ships at least . . .
Three times our total strength, not counting some,
Filling the port until the Fair has ceased.
Can you suppose, Sir, that they'll welcome us,
We, Corsair Lutherans, intruding thus?

'Not they, Sir, they will sink our ships on sight,
Burn all the Captains and enslave the crews,
The Spanish King believes he has the right,
And certainly the power, should he choose.
My word, Sir, is at all costs to be gone,
Northers or not, but never touch St John.'

'Frank,' Hawkins (may have) said, in kind reply,
'You take a gloomy view, as younglings will;
That Spanish boatswain with the bandaged eye,
Says the St John port must be empty still.
He saw the Fleet in Cuba . . . I maintain
Before it comes, we shall be gone again.'

'Sir, as your officer, I must decline
To trust that Spaniard, for his mates all swore
The Fleet had filled fresh-water, a sure sign
That they were sailing west in one day more.
I say, they will be there, when we arrive,
Or thereabouts, whatever we contrive . . .

'Consider, Sir, should we be in the port,
When the Fleet comes, what can we dare to do?

Defiance means a war with Spain in short,
With rope for me and headsman's block for you.
Acceptance means, a dawn of doleful doubt
And all our throats cut ere the day is out.'

'Frank,' Hawkins (may have) said, 'in such a case,
Civilized folk foregather and agree
Civilized ways in which to share the place,
In such a case such courtesy must be.'
'And how command your "courtesy" and "must"?'
Drake answered, 'I suppose by putting trust.'

'Yes . . . putting trust, upon a plighted word,
Or solemn oath, with hostages exchanged,
Fair promise upon Holy Writ averred,
Conditions sworn to, publicly arranged.'
'Yes,' Drake replied, 'one knows what trust men fix
When twenty highway robbers deal with six.'

'Frank, we are traders, with a licence signed
By the Queen Majesty's most Royal Hand,
A licence of much power, you will find,
Throughout these myriad miles from English land.'
'Sir,' Drake replied, 'let be . . . I only know,
Throughout this Main we have not found it so.'

Thus, possibly, they talked, as their ships neared
St John, and saw no signs of Fleet arrived,
No flags, no Fair, no coloured tents appeared,
But port and isle just honey to be hived,
They turned the Spaniards out and took possession,
And ruled there, as sea-kings, a little session.

The negroes hooked the anchors to the grips,
The sails were furled; the water-casks refilled,
A watch was set in batteries and ships,
And song by song the happy singing stilled.
All that had been had been as Fortune willed,
All things to come would be as Fortune wrought.
When morning dawned a new day would be brought.

III
The Port of San Juan de Ulloa

What was this port St John where Spanish slaves
Each autumn loaded goods from Mexico?
An islet three feet high above the waves
With some old chapel and a hut or so,
Fringing a gully where big ships could go
Packed side by side, with anchors hooked to rings.
Shelter and depth were its important things.

This depth and shelter made the place a port.
The City, Vera Cruz, was five leagues thence,
On the Main land with garrison and fort,
In year long tropic heat annulling sense,
In slow eternities of deadly summers,
While yellow-fever tested the new-comers.

As for St John, men had improved the scene,
Bringing fresh-water from a distant lake,
Smoothing a jetty where a reef had been,
And certainly the Gulf had fish to take.
For all things else it made the spirit ache,

And the mind sicken, and the heart despair
Until the Fleet came with September Fair.

Then the Coast wakened, and the colours flew,
Triumphant cannon fired, and bells pealed,
Bright tents were pitched, and there was much to do,
As New Spain sent Old Spain her season's yield,
The priceless emeralds in packets sealed,
The pearls, the silver bars, and the untold
Undreamed-of heavy splendour of pure gold.

Within the month, the fleet had left the Coast,
The harbour sheds were left, the guns laid low,
Beach, isle and port again looked like a ghost
In death until eleven months should go,
The sea-birds screamed the horror sea-birds know,
And day by day there burned the tropic sun,
On Saint John's port, then the Gulf's only one.

IV

The Spanish Fleet arrives at St John

'*What could you do, should foes appear*
At any point, in force, and near?
If you can surely answer this,
Your force's post is not amiss.'

To seawards distant lights of ships appeared . . .
The morning showed the Spanish fleet at length.
Still far away, but to St John's it steered,
All ships of war and more than thrice their strength.

And now it fell to Hawkins to explain
That he possessed the port and would remain.

He wrote as one possessing port and isle,
But holding them as mariners in need,
That clear conditions against force and guile
Must be discussed between them and agreed;
And hostages exchanged, and friendship vowed
Before their entering port could be allowed.

He could not know that in the Fleet he saw
Came the New Viceroy governing New Spain,
King Philip's proxy, giver of all Law
King absolute in all the Western Main.
And Hawkins' words were worse than writ in vain.
The Viceroy read, beneath St James's banners,
And said 'This Luther's dog shall be taught manners.'

Should he, the Viceroy, representing there
Of Europe's greatest House, the greatest Son,
The mighty Emperor Charles's son and heir,
About whose birth so many stories run . . .
Why, when the little Philip saw the sun,
The Emperor took horse and rode the ring,
Alone, and killed the bull in thanks-giving.

Should he . . . the great King's proxy, discuss terms
With one a Lutheran and corsair both?
The dog who asked it should be food for worms
Dead without root for any second growth
He would declare his friendship upon oath,
But pacts with Lutherans were not for keeping,
Such seeds were tares, that he would put to reaping.

And ordering his Navy to heave-to
He called a Council to discuss the ways
Of old deceits that might be used anew
Under all sweet—and softness that betrays,
The sun had hardly cleared the morning haze
When he had ordered troops from Vera Cruz
A picked two companies of force and youth.

PART TWO

I

The haggling about leave to enter the harbour
The Cousins speak

The Spanish fleet came to the St John Road,
Saluted and saluting: a great force . . .
And there they came to anchor and abode,
While long debate of captains took their course . . .
And much the Spaniards dreaded, where they lay,
Lest the time's Northers should arise and slay.

And much (no doubt) one watchful son of Devon,
Hoped that the stars might send such 'dew of Heaven'.

Hawkins, commanding had to make the choice,
To let the Spaniards in, or keep them out.
'I say, Defy them,' was his Cousin's voice.
'If not, they will destroy us, never doubt.
You cannot trust this Fleet and proxy King,
Placed as they are, they will swear any thing.

'We have been pirates here, seizing the place,
You owe it to all hands to save our lives,

We hold the anchorage by Heaven's grace,
Our poor throat's only shield from Spanish knives.
You hold them in a cleft stick: keep them there . . .
Whatever oaths of friendship they may swear.

'Remember, too, that being pirates here,
For such we are, our lives are confiscate,
By law of every nation far and near.
Once safe in harbour here they will not wait,
But swing us in some noose of no return,
All except you, but you they'll surely burn.'

'You have but to be firm; one Norther's rage
Will end their fleet, not you; they'll go ashore,
Done with salt water and the salt sea's wage,
And you at peace, much safer than before.
As for a war with Spain, we were here first,
And can remain here, let them do their worst.'

'Frank,' Hawkins (may have) said, 'in a Queen's ship,
I come here in distress, in dire need,
With all my squadron's standing gear to strip,
And full four hundred men and slaves to feed.
I pay for all I take, and only seek,
To stay perhaps five days, perhaps a week.

'As I command the port . . . (command I do,
They cannot enter till I give them leave),
I name the terms to be assented-to
Before I yield a jot that they receive.
The Viceroy must make oath to keep the terms.'

'No biting,' says the corpse, to the grave's worms.

II
The swearing of the peace

After three days debating, peace was sworn,
The Spanish fleet should enter and be moored,
With solemn oath and blowing of the horn,
Declaring endless love and peace assured.
The English squadron, Spain's beloved guest
Was, in all friendship, welcome to the West.

Hawkins and all his friends, should freely trade
Their cloth, their goods, their slaves; should buy and sell,
Like brother Spaniards, now that peace was made;
Viceroy and Hawkins swore that all was well . . .
The great King's proxy kissed his English brother . . .
As righteousness and peace they kissed each other.

Then, towards sunset, with salute of guns,
All colours flying; trumpets adding cheer,
The muscles of a thousand mothers' sons
Shortly to die, were singing at the gear,
Ship after ship hove slowly in with grace
Of a sea-bird to her appointed place.

III
On Wednesday the 22nd of September, 1568

It took two days to range and rearrange
Some thirty ships within that narrow dock
One feature of the order did not change,
Between the fleets lay twenty yards of rock.
This three-foot hillock helped them to divide,
The fleets apart; the ships were side by side.

As I suppose, the English held the Right
And Spain the Left of this long crowded space,
Each ship's head anchored to an iron bight,
Fixed on the only jetty in the place.
Our four small vessels at the Roadstead's lip,
The *Minion* next, and, inmost, Hawkins' ship.

Then, to the Left, beyond the shipless berth,
The next ship was the Spanish Viceroy's Flag,
The proxy of the greatest King on earth,
Bearing his scutcheon with its royal brag,
Then ship on ship, the Royal Fleet's array,
Preparing war tomorrow at mid-day.

And now that they were anchored and in force,
In swarms, in boats, on missions to and fro,
They showed the spirit of the scutcheon's horse,
That Spain deserved another world or so,
And yet, we know not if it seemed to any,
That they were very near and very many.

We know not what the English seamen thought,
Nor what they did and said: a seaman's day,
In any ship, brings matter to be wrought,
That must be done, ere work be put away.
Drake must have thought, seeing the setting sun,
That war was near, and foemen four to one.

Though the world darkened, and the watch was set,
Few Spaniards seemed to sleep: men were astir,
The midnight came, but they were working yet,
A berth was changed, and men, in shifting her,

Made a great noise close to the English line.
Carpenter noise, repairing some design.

Near as it was, they knew not what was doing
Some sailor's task after long days at sea,
Some inboard vital task of plank renewing,
Due to be done ere sailing home could be.
Many who heard, and toiled there until light,
Were to sleep very soundly before night.

IV
Thursday, the 23rd of September, 1568
Dawn till the forenoon

When daylight came, the English noticed much.
Much had been altered, not for any good,
A claw seemed to be ready for a clutch,
The shadow of a wolf showed in the wood,
A great hulk had been shifted from her rank
Near to our flagship on the English flank.

She was, perhaps, a berth where seamen slept
When their own ships were on their sides careening;
Or harbour store-house with no masting steppt
Her altered berthing seemed without a meaning
Though sailors' doings go by sailors' laws,
That favour nothing troublous without cause.

Why should the hulk be there, why should her side
Be seamed with alterations covered close,
Perhaps with gangways to be opened wide,

34

For boarders or for guns, if need arose?
And why, in Spanish ships, did cannon muzzles
Point to John Hawkins' flagship? these were puzzles.

Still, life is life, a day has its routine,
Men played the colours up, and stood bare-headed,
While Captains offered prayers for England's Queen,
While sea-birds cried and tidal waters eddied,
Then men dismissed to work, feeling uncertain
That all was well behind the Spanish curtain.

But, still, upon the whole, our men believed
That Spain would keep her promises of peace,
They had a mask of kindness that deceived,
And this, (part of the plotting) did not cease
This (part of the plan) had fullest play
In that grim morning of an evil day.

V

Of the Spanish plan

The plying of sentries and out-posts with drink; the killing of
Hawkins by a hostage; the hauling of the Hulk athwart the
Jesus *so that her hidden troops might board and take her; the*
total destruction of the English squadron

Doubtless, the purpose of the Spanish plan,
Was to deceive and then exterminate.
Make prize of every ship, kill every man,
And warn all Europe to avoid such fate.
But, till the moment of the sword, deceit
Should be the word and make the hour sweet.

Therefore the utmost cunning should be used
To tempt all leading hands like boatswains' mates
To liquor, until drunken or bemused
Neglecting gangs, or boats ashore, or gates.
So many loving-cups were given and taken
By breakfast, men were drunk and posts forsaken.

Then, they had planned that Hawkins should be killed,
Knifed by a hostage, at the outbreak's eve,
But in the *Jesus'* cabin Fortune willed,
A searcher found the dagger in his sleeve.
(Later, the Spaniards found him quite unharmed,
Down in the hold unfettered but disarmed.)

But the conclusion was to come at noon,
When the great hulk, dragged by a hundred hands
Should set the dance of sudden death in tune,
To bring the *Jesus* into Spain's commands.
Dragged athwart hawse her hidden crew would board
And put her men and master to the sword.

VI

About 10 in the forenoon Thursday, September 23rd, 1568

Now, as two thousand men were in the plot,
Symptoms of present peril were not few,
Cannon were being trained, with wadded shot,
Boats from ashore had musketeers for crew.
Some sentinels were drunk and singing catches,
Some Spanish gunners blew on lighted matches.

And little rudenesses increased the threat,
Of something evil getting out of hand,
Like distant sounds foretelling coming wet,
And jokes were cried that none could understand,
Unpleasant warnings in the morning sun
That they were hard at hand, and four to one.

And, presently, such boatloads of armed men
Came from ashore and landed on the isle,
With war-cries of 'Close, Spain,' and 'Tell us when,'
That none could doubt the imminence of guile . . .
Hawkins, who told the Viceroy what he feared,
Received a note of lies, as soon appeared.

For now, all Spanish cannon that could bear
On English ships, ran out, at point to fire;
The *Minion* judged it wise not to be there,
And find some harbour liker heart's desire;
She manned her outhauls, while the Sons of Sin
Aboard the hulk determined to begin.

It was full early, but they could not wait.
They hauled to board the *Jesus*, and let loose
The new-made gangways that were door and gate,
For the first charge at breaking of the truce,
The Viceroy, seeing this, bade trumpets blow,
For fire, sword and Hawkins' overthrow.

And, first, the main assault: three hundred men,
Crying 'Saint James' and 'Now close action, Spain,'
Rushed from the darkness of their devil's den,
To seize the English flagship or be slain.

All Spanish guns gave fire in support,
A rising cloud of battle hid the port.

As for our men ashore, marketing ware,
Or stewards buying victuals on the beach,
But two or three survived that Autumn Fair,
Swift sudden murder was the lot of each,
But for the great charge of the Spanish Foot,
The harvest reaped was very bitter fruit.

For, as a Ship of War, she was prepared,
Her seamen disciplined, her Captain cool,
Her close-fights death to enemies who dared,
Her gunners masters of a deadly tool,
That charge of foot a Dead Man's Welcome found,
Shot, blinded, piked, flung overboard and drowned.

Hawkins gave word to cut her anchor clear,
And man her after stern-fasts, hauling taut.
She swung athwart-wise between Road and Pier,
Meaning to join the *Minion* out of port.
But here, the Spanish fire held her fast.
King Henry's ancient ship had sailed her last.

And now the big brass cannon that defended
The Saint John anchorage, were manned and trained,
And heavy fire on her flank descended,
Gun after gun, and musket-bullets rained.
Tearing the rigging from her fenceless side,
And killing many men; but she replied.

Smoke dimmed the targets, but the fire heightened
How long, who knows? Who kept account of time?
But suddenly the Viceroy's flag-ship brightened,
Men saw a running fire from her climb,
Climb her high masts, and shrivel in its blaze,
All her proud stairways to her water-ways.

And there were cries and running from the flame,
But she was touchwood, and the fire roared,
And men were brave, but choking overcame,
And tongues of fire from her gun-ports poured,
And shooting ceased until with shattering thunder
Her fabric blew to pieces and went under.

VII
The end of Thursday, September the 23rd, 1568

After the thunder of the burst, the wreck,
Ruin of rigging, splinters, blocks and scraps,
All flinging sparks, rained on the *Jesus'* deck
And smoke blew by displaying the collapse.
The Spanish flagship sunk a blackened shell,
And two great Ships but wrecks, the stories tell.

As for the English fleet, the three small ships,
And the French friend were sunk to sail no more,
The *Jesus'* rigging was but tattered strips
Her stumps of masts their English colours bore.
Many lay dead aboard her, many maimed,
Her powder running short, her men untamed.

Then, in the battle's lull, her crew made shift
To screen the *Minion* with the *Jesus* frame,

And use that hour's quiet, Heaven's gift,
To light the day's disaster into fame.
Then, with cooled cannon made the Spaniards shun
The doubtful joy of fighting four to one.

And as she fought, the *Minion*'s men contrived
To salve her gear, her stores, her gathered gold,
The honey of their trade was safely hived,
(Save for some fifty slaves still in the hold).
Then that old ship still fired and made bold,
Till from the murk of smoke the end arrived.

Out of the fog of war blotting the haven,
Emerged two fire-ships, both blindly bound
To make more bodies pasture for the raven,
More corpses in the tide way with the drowned,
And seeing these all blazing, no defence
Could be (men judged) except to get from thence.

Nothing could save them but to leave the Flag,
(All those that could) and haul the *Minion* clear,
What sailors cannot carry they must drag,
And some poor souls had bitter dragging here.
Drake, in the *Judith*, rescued many men,
The bleakest minute of his life was then.

There in that port of death they left the wreck,
That triumph of old time, once Lubeck's pride,
Masts, yards, and rigging mangled on her deck,
With faint smokes rising from her shattered side.
The *Minion* and the *Judith* stood away,
The firing ceased, and darkness ended day.

VIII

East from St John
Drake alone

The Spaniards made no effort to pursue,
They had been sorely punished and refrained,
The *Minion* and the *Judith* slowly drew
Southward a mile, and there, awhile, remained.
They rove new gear, and sorrowed to the soul
At names unanswered when they called the roll.

There, doubtless by consent, the Kinsmen parted,
Drake, in his little overcrowded bark,
To sail five thousand miles of seas uncharted,
Hawkins to seek such landfall as the ark:
A rest he did not find, though he returned.
Half of his men far sadder endings earned.

For Drake, getting away, short of all stores,
There were grim thoughts and fortune more than grim.
Twelve hundred miles to sail by Spanish shores,
Threatening death for all, and fire for him,
And a wild ache for vengeance, yet no power,
To be avenged, put poison in the hour.

But ways to be avenged, not Hawkins' ways,
Came to his mind, with force and fiery tongue,
And he would find them not in many days
But soon, for all his life, and he was young.
And Spain should sorrow till his life was gone
Her breach of faith with England at Saint John.

Shame, at his Cousin's all too generous trust
Was nulled by feeling for his Cousin's pain.
Spain should atone for that in churchyard dust,
He would not serve, save in command again.
Fortune befriends the man who stands alone.
Fortune, his foe; yet Fortune should atone.

Another time Himself should be the guide,
Playing the gambits bidden by his star,
And not again be darkened and denied,
By men who trust where no foundations are.
Up, from the present darkness, he would climb . . .
Not thus would he return another time.

Thus in the night, seeing the helm relieved,
There, while a Norther blanched the Gulf like snow,
His Fortune told him and his soul believed
Of Spain in glory humbled and brought low.
Five thousand miles ahead lay Plymouth Hoe,
Above him, maddened topsail sheets were drumming.
He stood at con, the mate's watch went below,
He set the course ahead to glory coming.

NOTE

It had been one of John Hawkins's conditions that the two
contracting parties should exchange hostages. This had been
agreed, though with a reduction in the number to be exchanged.

One of the English men who wrote of the matter long afterwards, says that the Spanish hostages were not men of any account.
They were, however, accepted as such. The Spaniards found them

later, unharmed, in the battered hull of the flagship, the *Jesus of Lubeck*, after the action.

A Spaniard, writing from knowledge of the Spanish hostages at the time, says that some of them were not of very much account, but that some were men of position. Perhaps our own hostages were of no outward smartness after a year in the tropics in slave ships.

The English hostages were not harshly treated for two or three years, but were sent to Spain, where the Inquisition burned most of them. The English flagship was left in the harbour with some fifty living slaves still in the hold. She had been pretty well stripped before her men abandoned her. Perhaps some of the profits of the voyage reached England.

Drake, in the *Judith*, reached England four days before Hawkins. How he refitted and then kept the little ship afloat and provisioned in the autumnal North Atlantic is not told nor need to be told. He was a master mariner English Channel bred and his return proves it.

Later, in the years of his great success, jealous enemies blamed him for leaving Hawkins. We are not now jealous of Drake, but proud of him; and we need only say, that, at San Juan, Drake was under Hawkins's orders, in close touch with him, and both very well knowing the deadly danger in which they were. In any case, a Norther was coming on, and they had to part, for the *Judith* had to find, in the dark, a lee that she could lie in, or infallibly go ashore. Both the *Minion* and the *Judith* were full of weary, savage, men, many of them wounded, many of them having lost all their possessions, and all short of food, of water, and of hope, in ships that had been under fire all day, and now in an uncharted sea, at least a thousand miles from any safety and within three miles of a dozen big ships, each of greater power than they two combined.

I do not doubt for a moment that Hawkins counselled, if he did not order, the parting, and that Drake urged him to get out of the Gulf before food and water completely failed. This advice would have been tendered as from a kinsman, not as from a subordinate; and was ignored, or refused, with fatal results to many.

Both cousins were unusual: Hawkins, as a man of method, however laborious; Drake, as a man of genius. Sometimes the man of method must have been a trying commodore to his younger kinsman, whose ways were new to Time.

I have been asked what Drake did during the battle on September the 23rd.

We do not know, save that he was in the *Judith* loading survivors at the end of the day. One can suppose that the two cousins were not pleased with each other.

The *Judith* was a small bark, but was not sunk in the port like the other three small English vessels. Perhaps she was used by Drake in the Roadsted, to stop the coming of troops from Vera Cruz, or any movement of boats there.

This would have been work after his heart, and perhaps might have helped to make possible the great losses that the Spaniards (long afterwards) admitted.

Drake never forgot their breach of faith, and, in time, exacted some millions worth of damages.

PART THREE

You rest there under the sea
Ploughed still by English keels.
And so, farewell, brave hearts.

Long since, I travelled west, from port to port,
Along the Papal Grant, King Philip's Spain,
And saw, beyond the headland, once the fort,
Nombre de Dios steaming in the rain.

It was a manless forest, streaming wet
Empire endures but for a winter day.
The suns of then (a wonder once) had set.
Hawkins and Drake are buried in the bay.

Somewhere among the corals under sea
Swaying to pulses in the ocean's heart
Are those two cousins who could not agree
In unknown miles a half-inch on a chart.

The very half-inch very much in doubt . . .
We dipped our colours to them, thereabout.

SO THE MATTER RESTS

Below the glow-worms' hillock, in the grass,
A strange brown square of witheredness there was,
Like markings left at what was once a well;
What caused the blemish nobody could tell.

But after wandering allotted miles
By sea and land, in Fortune's frowns and smiles
I came to one eight thousand miles away
With photographs, of a much earlier day,
Showing the same spot, with the same dark square.
I asked the man, 'What are the markings there?'

He said 'They puzzled me . . . they puzzle you.
I often asked, but no one ever knew.'

JOYS

'What is Life's greatest joy?' I asked the sage,
He paused to think his thrilling moments through.
Then said, 'It changes between youth and age;
But this is certain Being Born Anew.'

True . . . I have known no rapture so intense
As resurrection for ten summer weeks
In Liverpool after long absence thence
In peace on earth such as the Christian seeks.

I was at rest among familiar faces
My savings waning fast, but O the joy
Of being welcome in beloved places,
With crumbs of hope left, being still a boy.

The savagery (I knew) would soon resume,
But O the joy of having left the tomb.

THINKING IT OVER

The soul is what the soul has won;
And Life is to enhance the soul:
Love fences every woman's son,
And at each barrier pays the toll,
Our lives pass like the leaves,
But each, who earns, receives.

GIVE WAY

'Give way, my lads,' the coxwains used to say
Bossing the crew and thinking themselves clever,
'So toss her up and splash me not with spray . . .
Give way.'

Then, out across the Sloyne or down the bay
The cutter made the water walls dissever,
The seagulls mewed above us in their play.

All earthly ill surrenders to endeavour,
Every tomorrow is another day,
All irons that seem barriers for ever
Give way.

THE DUMB THING'S VOICE

How can a flesh-imprisoned soul contrive
To think her message to a chosen friend?
How can man dead impress the man alive
By word or presence after his life's end?

Across a mapless world that no eye sees,
Across the pathless sea where no guides wait,
Across all frontier-posts where sentries be,
She finds direction and an open gate.

Thousands of miles she travels without bar,
How helped, we cannot know, but marvel much,
To where the love and understanding are,
That commune without word, greet without touch.

There the dumb pilgrim makes her message known,
By inspiration burning to the bone.

Men from the outer Channel Lights have told,
How birds of passage, dazzled by the glare,
Of the great lamps that guide the ships to fold,
Beat themselves dead in many hundreds there.

Thus, on a stormy mind, may spirits beat
Panting for light, believing light will cure
Even despairers, changing grim to sweet,
Rehearten life and make the footing sure.

Ah, happy those whose inner instincts guide
To the hid door with neither lock nor bar,
The saving door, that, knocked on, opens wide
And shows the midnight beautiful with stars.

The stars that bless, the order that prevails
Over all wreck and staunches all that ails.

What are the hunger and the thirst of souls?
An infant's outcry of the Being's need,
The Want unspeakable that naught controls,
Want of the very Being, Want indeed.

An agony of self, a wordless cry,
Sometimes with instinct who can give it aid
A thought, a cheer, a light to travel by,
Even the counsel, not to be afraid.

All this the Want has unknown strength to seek
Across the world, if need be, to the One,
The only One, and, though it cannot speak
Tells him the Want in language heard by none.

Such power has human Want, such guide, such wings,
It finds the longed-for harp and strikes the strings.

NATURE'S MEMORY

Long since, far hence, within a garden-close,
I talked with one who often saw the past,
A past, long dead, how long nobody knows,
A show, (no more) that left no cheek aghast.

A show of monks, where monks dwelt long ago,
Tilling the quiet scene with rake and spade,
Until some unheard signal made them go
In rank, away, elsewhere and swiftly fade.

She knew them all by sight, knew them as good,
In some strange way their goodness blessed the place
Precisely, why, she never understood
But something in them gave the ground a grace.

Much as in fields a strange bright flower or two
Shows later passers where a garden grew.

REMEMBERED GREAT ONES

All country workers had that look of might
All had done work removed from mortals now
The sixteen hour day, from dawn till night
In red clay country terrible to plough.

All had reaped corn with sickles, and mown hay
With scythes for ever shrieking, being whet,
Some for their feats are chronicled today
By pious record in a chancel set . . .

How one, within a day, had threshed with flail
(A task still thought the hardest man can do)
A mighty weight of corn and quotes the tale,
A near-by bracket keeps the flail in view.

The bones of such men people unknown cells
Close to each church where once they rang the bells.

SITTING ALONE

Sitting alone, far hence, in summer night,
Watching the fireflies and reading verse,
Or ignorantly seeking how to write,
Changing each chosen master for a worse.

O how I longed for someone who had read
Even one book of poems to its end,
Had noted what was living and what dead,
And could encourage, not condemn, a friend.

And he, (at work, four thousand miles away,)
Told me, long afterwards, that I had been
A haunting to him, ever, night and day,
A wonder to him, what the fact might mean.

He, thinking I had died, he knew not where
Of my great want of him was well aware.

OLD ENGLAND

Just half a century since, an old man showed
Some photographs of forty years before,
Of timber carters in a country road
The very people, in the clothes they wore.

There they appeared; the nation now extinct,
Survivors from before the Flood they seemed,
Horses and carts such parts of them, so linked,
That they were one, a trinity undreamed.

A trinity in unity of power
To tomm the oak-tree into human use,
Or with a twitched ring make a bull to cower,
Or, grinning, turned the shire stallion loose.

Such might was in them they were hardly men,
Those prehistorics peopling England then.

A MEMORY OF A SINGER

Long since, after the weary war, you came
East, from the Cotswolds to me, there to sing
Poems of yours and ballads of old fame,
Many a moving, many a merry thing.

I thought of Blake, the English Lad who sang
To tunes too beautiful for tongue to tell;
Of Allingham, whose country ballads rang
Where Irish brooks a winding river swell . . .

And of old poets, long-forgotten now,
Who, after singing, left, in country ears
Notes, that were comfort in the time of tears,
Words, that directed furrows at the plough.

Themselves, perhaps, but memory of a tone
Of mirth, of sadness, never heard again,
An unseen thing, that like a fallen rain,
Or vanished sunshine, kindled a seed sown.

CHURCHYARD CHEER

They are all underneath the grass
Forgetting what the trouble was.

Whatever wickedness they wrought
Is out of Time, and Life and Thought.

The score upon the Slate is cleansed
The outraged have been recompensed,

And they are underneath the grass,
Forgetting what the trouble was.

PAGAN-BORN or
THE THREE-DAY DEATH

PART ONE

I

They used to tell me stories of a Prince
Of some old dreaded tribe on Wicked Hill,
In pagan England, many ages since
Fragments of stories, half-remembered still;

How he, becoming Christian, was expelled
From all his Father's fiefs, and made his way,
West over Severn to where Christians held,
Hoping for Christian care and leave to stay.

But near the Severn ford his way was barred,
'What is this scion of a pagan king
Entering Christian earth for?' asked the guard.
'Alone; at dawn, too; an unheard-of thing.'

Some sought to turn him back, yet had the grace
To send him to the Reeve, to hear the case.

'The Reeve,' they said, 'will know what can be done.
Under the old Reeve you'd have been refused.
All of your kingdom, every Mother's Son,
Before these modern softnesses were used.

'The present Reeve is at the inn below.
He must decide your case; so take him west.
We do not love your kingdom, as you know,
We do not like such cuckoos in the nest.'

They marched the lad in guard, over the pass,
Under the steepness, down the slope beyond,
Scaring the rabbits in the dewy grass,
Pausing to drink at Fortune's spring and pond.

Below there, at the inn, was whom they sought
The King's Reeve, new to office, deep in thought.

The Reeve received the lad, dismissed the guard,
And finding pleasure in unusual cases,
Gave to this case his most intense regard,
Seeing its impact upon tribes and places.

And though the face and manner of the youth
Pleased, like his tale of suffering for faith,
Yet looks mislead, and stories lack in truth
And Reeves, misled and cheated may have scathe.

Might not an angry father chase his son,
Demand him, as a prisoner escaped,
With much ill will, and border raids begun?
So, in the young Reeve's mind, the matter shaped.

So the young Reeve, new come to task and scene,
Judged what the coming of the lad might mean.

Some novel plot of pagan trouble East
Added to all the trouble in the South,
So that the trouble West might be increased
And ginger be made hotter in the mouth.

But could it be that on his Severn border
Away to Southward, in the lawless Wild

Were outlaws joining to the pagan order,
And causing trouble through this Christian child?

The pagans and the godless joined together
Helping the fury of the men of Wales,
Would bring his Reeve-ship into heavy weather,
With trouble to all peace, and shortened sails.

The boy looked innocent, but what are looks,
To him, all pagans born were hawks or rooks.

Then, too, the pagan father of this son,
The King on Wicked Hill, was an old foe,
A warrior pagan and an evil one,
Cause of much ill, not very long ago.

All this he wondered as he faced the lad,
And said, 'Few fathers can be angry long . . .
Surely, he'll soon forgive you and be glad.
And prove more kind for having done you wrong?'

'No,' the boy said, 'I've hurt him to the core
He never will forget it, nor forgive.
And I am certain that he'll nurse the sore
And let the poison rankle while I live . . .

'He would have killed me in his temple there
Had not his Council prayed him to forbear.'

The Reeve
'Though east of Severn you must surely know
Of the lost wilderness that borders this.

Should we reject you, do you think to go,
To settle there? A godless place it is?'

The Prince
'No, Sir, our people seldom enter in
To that wild land, and suffer if they do.'

The Reeve
'Some, in the past, have planned and fostered sin,
There, in the recent past; and might not you?'

The Prince
'No, Sir, because this last Midsummer Day,
My Brother went there, on some folly bound.
They tortured him with wisps of burning hay,
And staked him in the Severn till he drowned.

'So never think my House makes one with them.
How came a people there, whom all condemn?

'We think them Christians, but how came they thus?
I often ask, and ask, with no reply.
Your next-door neighbours, bordering on us,
Are enemies to all men; tell me why.'

'Sir,' the Reeve said, 'In the great pestilence,
The Three-Day Death, their wickedness began.
All that estate to twenty miles from hence,
Was left unpeopled, killed, without a man.

'Churches, religious houses, farms and homes,
Towns, all deserted, peopled by the dead,
The hills a waste where now the wild bull roams,
And no man left for whom Christ's blood was shed.

61

'I only tell the tale men told to me . . .
The tale explaining how things came to be.

'Into this desert where the dead folk lay
Came outlaws, lepers, madmen, many a score,
Who seized the dead mens' havings as a prey,
And pirates landed upon Severn shore.

'The few wild wandering children who survived
(Gangs of young murderers, so stories tell)
They tamed or killed; and so the state arrived,
The human ruin lapsed into a hell.

'Such is the story . . . I believe it true,
The Death was the great cause of what we know,
The Wild's a hell I hunger to make new
To plough afresh with better seed to sow.'

'Sir,' the boy said, 'May Heaven help your scheme,
And may I help to make it more than dream?'

The Reeve
'So I must hope; at present, Southern Wales,
Threatens our borders, and the Wild must wait
But the Wild's wildness overtips the scales,
With all the insolence that brings a Fate.

'Eleven parish churches without priest,
And four religious houses without men,
An Earl's commandery where law has ceast,
And man is but a wolf-pack in a den.

62

'It is full time; and in the nick are you . . .
A King's son, outlawed for religion's sake . . .
Like sunrise brightening the morning dew,
A bell of morning, bidding men awake.

'You come, in pagan blood-feud, with this horde
Yet trust to God to heal them, not the sword.

'I think that you might help me in the task . . .
Some little leaven could be found and tried.
Be ready, then, to help me when I ask.
We'll seek to heal this wounded countryside.

'For you, I welcome you to stay with me,
The King, your Father, shall be made aware
And if he claim you, it will have to be . . .
My orders are conclusive, so beware.

'And, mind, no word of this, for spies exist
The Wild is near and what is heard is told.
And what is whispered in the morning mist,
May scare the Wild before the day is old.

'But I accept your presence: now away . . .
You must come with me; I go West today.'

Horses were saddled, and away they rode
Through miles of cattle-pasture stretching west
Where white-faced cattle glared at them and lowed,
The Reeve in happy converse with his guest,
They startled many a partridge from her nest,
And passed by many a church whose bells were sweet
Above the trample of their horses' feet.

II

At Hereford, the Bishop took the lad
Into his train; the Reeve bade him farewell,
Smoothing his passage with what wealth he had,
Then riding to the March where wars befell.

The Bishop pled with Wicked Hill in vain.
'The pagan king abjured his Christian son,
Let Christians love him, pagans would abstain
In pagan lands the Prince's day is done.

'Since Christians seemed to like him, let them keep,
May Woden give them joy of such a prize.
Pagans disliked the staggers in their sheep.'
(The Bishop read the bitter words with sighs.)

'Let Christian shepherds guard their silly stock,
Lest the lad's staggers decimate their flock.'

So some months passed, till the Prince made a plea
To be allowed to venture in the Wild,
If only to attempt to know and see,
But bringing hope of being reconciled.

'Surely,' he pleaded, 'I could venture in
With some small donkey-cart of peddler's ware,
For surely some such barter must begin
Some day or other, with the people there.'

'But no,' the Bishop said, 'your Brother's fate
And other tales as grim, plainly forbid
Any such sort of trial: we must wait,
For fairer weather, as the cuckoo did.

'I see your eagerness and how you chafe,
But all my people think it too unsafe.'

But as time passed, his eagerness increased,
He sought to quell his pagan sense of feud,
Its vengeances forbidden by the priest,
Its bloodsheds, each the parent of a brood.

And as, in time, the iterated drop
Wears out a channel in the mountain stone,
So the lad's plea annulled the prelate's stop,
Permission came, that he might go alone.

He, with a little load of tempting store,
Might try to barter in the Wild, in trade,
For such might prove the opening of a door,
He might be right . . . beginning might be made.

In happy triumph the lad went in haste
To purchase goods for barter in the Waste.

But though he had permission, he was sure
That such permission might be set aside,
Warning might come of evil without cure
And special risk in that lost countryside.

And he being but young believed that youth
Knew better than a Bishop what to dare,
He said that he would go, and told the truth
But told no living Christian how or where.

He made his preparations in hot haste
Telling no person what his course would be,

65

And at a daybreak entered to the Waste
With none to wish him fortune, and none see.

At daybreak on the trackless grass he crosst
The known but unseen frontier of the lost.

Youth makes the great decisions knowing naught
Of what they cost the maker, being made.
This youth was overwhelmed with generous thought
And did with joy what generous feeling bade.

How he should barter, was not wholly clear,
That he could trade at all was most uncertain,
To untried youth the untried thing is dear,
Youth longs to see and know and cut the curtain.

Blithely the princely pedlar trod the grass,
His donkey-paniers full of cups and knives,
Platters and honey, mead and hippocras,
Caps for the men and kerchiefs for their wives.

Salt, mustard, onions, toys of little cost
And russet apples that had stood the frost.

Some miles away, upon a likelier route
The Bishop's guards hurried to stop his going
With urgent word to follow in pursuit,
A warning having come of tempests blowing.

Of merry-making of the devil's kind
Within the Waste a Satan's holiday
The guards, as ordered, sought but could not find,
Nor any symptom of the Prince's way.

66

Meanwhile the Prince, some miles away, was making
A path from safety to a rude awaking.

III

There the Wild lay before him, hills and woods,
The orchard trees, with pear and cherry white.
To the left, wooded hills, and to the right
Hills, and some smokes, and unknown solitudes.

Some gleams of water shone; a ruined spire
And broken-windowed church were near at hand,
No song of work or folk seemed in the land.
The ruins of the church were black with fire.

He passed the church, he held over a brook,
He heard a distant sound of water falling,
Over the Wild were many cuckoos calling,
Over the elm trees called the nested rook . . .

There was no sign of living man, no sound,
Of work or play; no footprint in the ground.

There, among bushes, one had lain in wait
And maimed or killed a little roving lad
For broken partridge eggs and what he had.
What breed of pike had risen to such bait?

What bare-foot bandit had not missed the shoe?
The shoe of a small boy, whose body lay
Stripped in a boggy patch some yards away,
In mud, forget-me-not and morning dew.

There the poor little child lay in the mud,
And here the Prince, in horror, stopped and prayed.
And knew how terribly Death makes afraid
And how appallingly blood calls for blood.

Then on, he went, for there was water falling
There to his left, and were not people calling?

Then suddenly, he saw a creature stand,
A ghost of ruin, in that haunted waste
A ragged thing that gabbled and grimaced,
Munching some knops of nasty from her hand.

Woman, perhaps, but liker a sick beast
With dandelions in her towselled locks,
Something between a hedge-hog and a fox,
With sauce-alone as salad to her feast.

'Gah-gah', she snarled, fearing he came to steal
The hare-form of her harbour in the ditch,
She flung a stone, and cursed him like a witch,
And sped away clutching her filthy meal.

Such were his lot, a mad thing, a dead child,
His springtime's morning welcome to the Wild.

Soon afterwards the noise of water grew,
A splash of water falling upon stones,
And there a ruin lay of old burned bones,
In which the marigolds were sprouting new.

There had been killing there, long long before.
And burning, too, and now, a falling brook

Splashed and broke bubbles, and the building rook
Up to an elm-tree top new timbers bore.

And here for the first time, not very near,
He heard, somewhere ahead, men shouting loud
Certainly men in some excited crowd
Now falling still anon arising clear.

Somewhere ahead, were those he sought to find,
The dreaded lost ones hardly human kind.

No one appeared, but plainly on ahead,
Many were gathered: and in fullest cry,
And now he had a path to travel by,
And smelt the smoke of houses where it led.

And as he went, the shouting, growing much,
Would roar into a tumult till it raged,
Then lapsed to tensenesses as skill engaged
And courage grew to put it to the touch.

Now mongrel yelpings sounded in the shouts,
And horns were blown, at some triumphant feat,
And metal gongs and wooden drums were beat,
The testing place and Death were thereabouts.

And in the Prince's mind the thought was drumming,
'Somewhere below those elm trees Death is coming.'

Rounding a bend, he came upon some huts
A village among fruit-trees white with bloom,
The dwellings all as silent as a tomb,
The paths untidy all and seamed with ruts.

Doors were left open, and some embers gleamed,
On hearths in places, but no person showed.
Pigs grunted, kennelled dogs barked, and cocks crowed,
The dwellers were in bliss elsewhere it seemed.

For further on, he heard a roaring crowd
Maddened with joy applauding luck or skill,
That dodged or parried something meant to kill,
The roaring hushed, and then again was loud.

There were the people of the Wild at play,
Satan and all his host on holiday.

In a few moments, there ahead, a space
All trodden, was a camp, as at a Fair,
Rude carts, with shafts uptilted in the air,
And mongrel tethered dogs to guard the place.

The horses were among trees, further on,
At posts, or rails, at nose-bag or at hay,
A ribby chuckleheaded lot were they,
But still, no living soul; the folk were gone.

But gone, not far, for though the bushes hid
Where the crowd was, some interest intense
With trampling, outcry, danger and defence,
Hinted of hell, and what they saw and did.

Outcries and tramplings, curses, sudden pauses
Told of souls desperate in dreadful causes.

Now, as he passed the carts, a roaring burst
From an enclosure near it, some dispute,

Or battle, rather, between brute and brute.
Gang against gang in frenzy hacked and cursed.

And instantly, the fighting crowd in fury
Was round him, and at once he was their prey,
Donkey and cart like dust were swept away.
The mob becoming Law and judge and jury.

He was knocked down, but dragged onto his feet
He saw his packets snatched, his donkey driven,
He heard the red law shout his judgment given . . .
The shout of 'Give him to the dogs to eat.'

Then, suddenly, a great voice shouted clear,
'Stop it, you fools, at once, and bring him here.'

A short man, of immense breadth, shouted this,
Town crier once, in a town dead of pest.
The roaring rabble let the victim rest
Like dogs obeying where a master is.

They dragged the lad into a timbered ring
A bull-ring, with dead bulls not cleared away,
And tossed dogs, not yet dead, kicking in clay.
There, in a bannered throne room sat their King.

Apart, within the ring, a butcher's gang,
Drew knives to flay the red bulls newly killed.
Dry blood-stains were the badges of their guild,
They nibbled bits of fat and cursed and sang.

Then the acute swift edge its harvest cropped.
The rabble faced the monarch's box and stopped.

The Prince looked at the King; and his heart sank,
This was the unfrocked priest who ruled the Wild,
An iron face with lips that never smiled
An iron heart from which his subjects shrank.

No mercy, and no beauty, and no joy
Was in the spirit that had wrought such face,
One glance sufficed for hearing of the case.
'So,' the King said, 'And this is the Reeve's boy.

'Listen, you scum, abandon brawling here.
Take this boy hence, and give him a fair start
And loose your dogs and run him like a hart
And munch his bones; then cast dice for his gear.'

Having so sentenced, and no answer made,
He ordered dinner, that had been delayed.

And instantly, giving no chance of speech,
The rabble seized the lad and dragged him thence,
A sentenced bundle almost without sense,
Battered and punched by any that could reach.

Into the open pasture they all ran,
Some fetching mongrel dogs, some seeking stones,
Or telling dogs 'Yes . . . you shall have his bones,
Sick him, good Towzer, catch him if you can.'

Up to a little grassy rise they went
A long stretch, thickly wooded, lay below.
A starter pushed him where he had to go
The dogs were brought to him to sniff his scent.

The starter said, 'When I say "Run, boy"', run.
Or you'll be dog's meat and your day'll be done.'

'Wait, now,' the starter shouted to the crowd,
'Keep back, to give him law: wait for the horn,
His sentence is to beat you or be torn.
A fair start of a hundred yards allowed.

Now, wait until the horn . . . Now run, boy, run.'
The boy, though nearly stripped, still had his shoes.
He ran at the command, he could not choose,
Straight for the woodland shining in the sun.

Ten terrified swift paces his mind told,
And then the horn blew and the dogs in cry
Were loosed, and on they came to make him die,
In some near five foot measure of hill mould.

Panting he ran as he had never run
In wild blind terror and his living done.

There, shockingly, by mongrel curs disjointed
He would have perished for the dogs and crows,
Among the harebells where the curlew goes,
But Death prevails by Destiny appointed.

And there in terror in the grassy space
Blinded with fear, and thinking himself dead
He roused a hare in form, who upped and sped
And Destiny contrived her saving grace.

She saved his life: the mongrels changed to hare
The rabble chased the pack with curse and cry

The Prince was left alone under the sky,
Where kestrels cruised or floated upon air.

He reached the woodland cover, while away
Far thence, the hare led men and dogs astray.

Beyond the wood, the land-marks were his guide,
He came to safety with a tale to tell
Of effort lost and intercourse denied
And devils doing devilry in hell.

He blamed himself for failing; he declared
That, somehow, still, he would discover ways,
Of lighting the Wild's darkness to a blaze
Of the great guiding light that must be shared.

Meanwhile, he would go seek, for seekers find.
The penny of himself was there to spend . . .
The morning follows soon on midnight's end,
A sparkle of a light was in his mind.

But, in that mind, great misery prevailed
That he, the chosen hand, had tried and failed.

PART TWO

The Bishop's guards blamed him for having crosst
Into the Waste without their full assent.
The stewards muttered at the donkey lost,
The dainties wasted and the money spent.

The Bishop blamed himself, but thought the lad
Had acted like a lad in too much haste
Which wisdom should have thought of and forbad,
Not giving thus a triumph to the Waste.

The Reeve wrote words of comfort, saying 'Son . . .
You were preserved by miracle most strange.
For greater future tests that will be won . . .
Defeats must be endured, for fortunes change.

'The hare that saved your life was sent to save,
Take courage, Fortune brightens to the brave . . .
I who write this in mud, in driving rain,
Can only say take courage, try again.'

As time went by, that heals so many ills
He was admitted to a clerkly school
Of monks and scholars in the middle hills,
And loved the place, the learning, and the Rule.

But mourned acutely as a young man mourns
For having failed in that so grim attempt
That promised balm, but ended amid thorns
In terror infinite and ill undreamt.

And much he sorrowed for old pagan friends,
Still there, he hoped, on Wicked Hill, alive . . .
And learned, as youth learns, how affection ends,
In dreams of joys that never can arrive.

That slowly cease to hurt biting apart
Their aching passage from a broken heart.

Then, being pagan-born he had to bear,
Much mockery for little things unknown,
Customs and manners differing everywhere,
Often (he thought) less pleasing than his own.

Much mockery of his Father and his kin
On that side Severn held by no means dear,
Such, if he answered, was accounted sin,
And if he answered not, accounted fear.

And spies were ever tempting him to speak
Some rash reply that they could quote aloud,
To make him a new nickname for a week,
And give a week of triumph to the crowd.

The Prior knew these tales, but said 'Let be . . .
The lad will come to something: wait and see.'

Meanwhile, the Reeve, in Wales, in conflict grim,
Battled far thence, a memory growing dim.

After some years, the young Prince deep in thought
Quitted the school, of mockery and blame,
And asked and asked and anguished and besought
For wisdom's answer, but no answer came.

All of man's ways and customs seemed about
To break in blood: a ship with scarlet sails,
Had come up Severn; an appalling rout
Had come, men said, upon the Reeve in Wales.

Nearer at hand the Wild with threat and curse
In raid on raid, had taken heavy toll,

And every blow that troubled threatened worse,
Till daily life was bitter in the soul.

Day after day the sun in a brass sky,
Burned, past belief, and grass began to die.

Northward and westward towards Wales he went,
Sick for his friend the Reeve reported killed,
He met with ragged fleers battle-rent,
Who told him whatso'er they thought he willed.

How the Reeve, at a daybreak, his horse lamed,
Himself sore wounded, with three men at most .
Was set upon at some Welsh ford un-named,
And fighting hard had given up the ghost.

'And now the Welsh,' they said, 'are streaming on,
Nothing to stop them, nothing, even, to check,
All Hereford is doomed and Shropshire gone,
All the Welsh Marches gone in utter wreck.

'Go you no further west, for they are coming,
Thousands, with banners flying and drums drumming.'

At dusk, numbed by these stories, he encamped
Among the rocks of Wrekin, looking down
Acres where still the wild white cattle stamped,
Dusts of dead Romans in their ruined town.

And there, as the night darkened the hot air,
Was confirmation of a conquering horde,
The fires of a vast camp made a glare,
The Welsh in triumph bringing fire and sword.

77

And here at the first glimpse of ruin's might
Came the first knowledge of undying power,
That makes the human spirit all delight
And with a song annuls the fatal hour.

'Those are the Welsh,' he said. 'But Wrekin stands
And Severn runs, and Teme, and God commands.'

At dawn, he hurried west and north for news,
And found the people crazy with alarms,
Fearing the worst and shaking in their shoes
Hiding in woods the cattle from the farms.

'As for the news, all news in war is bad,'
Somebody said, 'But sometimes there is food,
And, sometimes, sleep, but you, begone, my lad,
Get home to Gytha while the going's good.

'The Welsh have won the day, but a day passes,
They're on the march, no doubt, for where they plan,
And those who try to stop them now are asses,
So take a fool's advice; begone young man.'

So others spoke, and with swift cunning drove
To save their cows from being treasure trove.

So, much bewildered, back he turned, and sped,
A long day's tramp in heat to Squaymer's Pond,
Above whose gleam the beacon raised his head,
And cruising kestrels flitting shadows conned.

There, as he camped, a farm-hand setting snares,
Said that 'three scarlet ships had come from Hell,

Away, there, east, and called the Severn theirs,
And brought the Moorish Plague, so people tell . . .

'And, for the Wild, it comes to open war
To take sheep pasture from us, and new wives,
There'll be sad doings before summer's o'er
With these and all those Welshmen with their knives.

'Yes, and that pagan gang on Wicked Hill,
While all this murder thrives, they won't be still.'

He left, leaving his snares, and the night darkened,
The nightjars chirred, the owls a-mousing called,
Charming the little wits of mice that hearkened . . .
The Prince, then looking westward, was appalled.

For there, unlooked-for, a few miles away,
On Oster Hill, fire on fire showed . . .
The army of the Welsh in full array,
In the still night the sun-baked fuel glowed.

'Doubtless,' he thought, 'they come in settled plan,
To join my Father, by the Severn ford,
And call the Wild to join them every man,
Take what we have and put us to the sword.

'So then, tomorrow's sun may be the last,
That I shall see, and all my troubles past.'

Almost at once two horsemen, side by side,
Rode past him, where he lay, speaking no word
But pausing, near to listen as they spied,
And startling now and then some roosted bird.

79

'Out-riders from the camp; patrol sent out,
To seek their allies' outposts,' the Prince thought.
'Seeking my Father's spearmen without doubt,
Expecting danger here, and finding naught.'

He would have followed them, but there came sounds
Both east and west of users of the night,
Men bearing arms, not talking, going rounds,
Their bridle elbows wrapped in rags of white.

In a short quiet he arose and crept
Into thick woodland covert where he slept.

Slept, or half-slept, awakened by the stirs
Of hunted rabbits squealing in despair;
Of endless sorrow sighing in the firs,
And distant thunder in the midnight air . . .

Sleeping for very weariness at last,
But with ill-dreams of one without a place,
Born to great splendour in the pagan past,
Now scorned on every side and in disgrace.

Then he would waken for the very grief
Of being nothing, and condemned to naught,
A blighted bud that never would be leaf,
A shopman's broken toy that no one bought.

Dawn silvered Cotswold and the Severn gleamed,
Sleep overcame him and he dreamed; he dreamed.

First a confusion of contesting words
Like Do and Do not, in a doubtful cause,

Then, trumpets, axe-strokes and the cries of birds
Then myriad birds in flight, and then a pause.

And in the silence, lo, his Mother stood
His long-dead Mother, there, her very soul,
A thing of brightness to all deathly mood,
With wild white roses in her aureole.

'My son,' she said, 'I come out of the Now,
That ever Is, to bid you to be brave,
Light in your very soul shall tell you how;
All that is lost, yourself shall help to save.

'All that seems lost, yourself shall help restore,
A precious gold is in the rocky ore.

'Hope will sustain, for Hope pierces all death
To what is Life while earth and living are,
Therefore take Hope and breathe immortal breath,
And be, to God, a child, to men, a star.

'This very morning, you will face a man,
Face him in deadly peril of eclipse,
And tell him that his scope has had its span,
And ruin nears him, from the scarlet ships.

'And you, be of good cheer, for Time begins
To use you as a man who can perceive
Truth as a guide among Man's greeds and sins.
I know your want and bid you but believe.

'This is the morning of a turning tide,
Words will be given; Hope and Truth abide,'

Not far away, a slope was being cleared,
The timber cut, the roots out-dragged away,
A voice there shouted orders as he neared,
The voice remembered from that earlier day.

And pressing-on, he found the timber-hands,
Huddled aside, (their axes on the ground)
Scared at the great voice giving them commands,
Town-crier once, but now the Wild King's hound.

'Henceforth,' it shouted, 'all this chase is ours,
So I announce for Satan, the Wild's King.
Your laws, you will abjure, and obey ours,
Or taste whatever torment death can bring.

'So Satan bids, and here his spearmen stay
To wring the necks of all who disobey.'

The brightness dimmed away; he woke and stood,
No one was there, no foot-prints marked the dew,
But horse hoofs sounded southward in the wood,
The sky was all bright summer blazing blue.

The glory of the dream made his heart thrill,
A heavenly listener had heard his pleas;
But what was all this talk of coming ill
To deadly foes, and ships from over seas?

He knew that he would know within the hour
And that the knowledge would be test indeed.
The dream was Hope and Truth, and both are power,
And must prevail where courage sows the seed.

Then at the running spring he took for guide
That noise of horses near the cover-side.

And there some spearmen stood under their lord,
King Satan of the Wild crowned with soft gold
From some long-perished Briton's burial hoard,
The self-same King the lad had seen of old.

'So,' the King said, 'You hear, and therefore know
That instant death awaits all who dispute,
As long as Winter East Wind comes with snow,
As long as Spring brings grass, and Autumn, fruit.'

'Sir,' the Prince said, advancing man to man,
'Have you not heard what dire peril waits
There in the palace where your rule began,
The Death that treads within your very gates?

'The scarlet ships that threaten you and yours,
With sudden pestilence that nothing cures?

'Yes, and the Moorish Prince, who wooes your Queen,
Has won your Queen, as mistress and has gone
Making your might a tale of what has been,
And you a mock for boys to jest upon.

'Yes, and the scarlet ships that took her thence
Have left a three-day death that smites men dead
The fatal oriental pestilence,
By which, even now, your dogs are being fed.

'All this your Speaker knows; he saw it kill
Before he came to join your foray here.

You, Speaker, tell him as you can and will,
Before you know the Death now drawing near.'

He ceased, and eyed the man with the great chest,
Now white as chalk, in trouble manifest.

He staggered forward, paused, and cried, 'Hear all,
The lad tells truth, three scarlet ships from Hell,
Anchored five days ago at evenfall,
For slaves to buy and silks and gems to sell.

'And there they bought your Queen, that crazy girl,
For more than she was worth, a yellow dress
All spangled up with amethyst and pearl
Long since the wearing of a Moor Princess.

'She wore it, and away to sea she went
Good riddance to us all; but two ships stayed
Men, gear and ships alike their poison sent,
And swift death followed all who tried to trade.

'I saw them die . . . but your command was clear,
To claim this Chase as yours, and I am here.

'I say the man tells truth, your day is done,
Why, the good lack, I hear the horses' feet,
Trampling to end whatever you've begun,
Before the growing corn is bread to eat.

'I, who was Crier in a Market Town,
Telling of trinkets lost and cattle strayed,
See the green leaf but not again the brown . . .
I have the three-day death, my part is played.

'I have the three-day death . . . I who once cried
(I who once sang in quire) a great bass,
"Lost, strayed or stolen" along Severn side,
Tell you, you're done, and tell it to your face.

'So ho, my lovely hounds . . . go seek, go seek'
He staggered and fell dead, ceasing to speak.

Then, in the hush death brings, a tramp of horse
Rang in the wood, a horseman's bugle blew,
Cavalry closed that forest-end in force,
The Reeve with all the stalwarts of his crew.

The Reeve triumphant, having earned a peace
Returned to end the Wild with all it claimed.
Swift horsemen made their Satan's babble cease,
To wait for fitting trial and be tamed.

And there, the Bishop, was calling for men,
To fight the three-day death before it spread,
And make its wild asylum sane agen,
And many stalwarts joined him as he pled.

But now a messenger arrived at speed
Crying, 'My lord and Bishop: news indeed.

'The King of Wicked Hill with all his knights
Being warned by dream and omens to amend,
Seek Christian Baptism with all its rites
At Severn Ford, that war between us end.

'He seeks to see his Son, now become heir,
To all he has; he undertakes to build

What churches lack, if you will tell him where,
He will endow them and will see them filled,

'He asks moreover to be granted leave
To build new churches in the ruined Wild,
That bells may call to prayer at dawn and eve,
And faith restored where life has been defiled.'

'O Sir,' the Bishop said, 'Let us all hence,
To end all war, all Wild, all pestilence.'

So it was done, in that old day of June,
Between the Chase and Severn before noon.

From the volume

LYRIC INTERMEZZO

by

HEINRICH HEINE

(*22*)

If the little flowers could know it,
How deep is my spirit's pain,
They would weep as my little brothers,
To give me my heart again.

If the nightingales could know it,
My sorrow so sick and strong
They would gladly make for my healing
At once, reviving song.

If the gold-speckt stars in Heaven
Could hear of my woe, or see,
They would come down from Heaven,
And put a new hope in me.

But they do not know; they cannot.
But One, the secret knows,
She knows, who did the breaking,
How broken my heart goes.

(*58*)

October scatters the apples,
I'm wrapped in my grey hood,
In a night dripping and bitter
I ride alone in the wood.

87

And, riding so, there, with me,
My thoughts, too, ride the ways.
They lead me, lusty and light-foot,
To where my darling stays.

The dogs are barking, the servants
Bring candles that flare and blink;
Climbing the stairs, impatient
My spurs on the floorings clink.

In the bright-lit, tapestried chamber
(So sweet and dear is the place)
There, waiting, is my beloved,
I rush into her embrace.

Still storms the wind in the branches,
Thus speaks the Oak, I deem:
'What would you, O crazy rider,
With your more crazy dream?'

(*64*)

Night was upon my eyelids,
Lead was upon my lips,
Annulled in mind and spirit
I lay in the grave's grips.

How long I cannot tell you
I lay there stunned and dead,
I woke . . . someone was knocking
My tombstone, overhead.

'Will you not rise, dear Henry?
It's now un-setting sun,
The dead are up, re-living,
Eternal Life's begun.'

'I cannot rise, my darling,
I'm blind, and must be blind,
My eyes, from so much weeping,
Are withered out of mind.'

'But I will kiss them, Henry,
Kiss all their night away . . .
And you shall see the Angels,
And all the Star's array.'

'I cannot rise, my darling,
I bleed . . . I'm bleeding still . . .
Where you, to my heart, struck me
The sharp word that could kill.'

'See, Henry; I lay lightly
My hand where hurt remains . . .
Then it will bleed no longer,
And healed be all my pains.'

'It cannot be, my darling,
All shattered is my head,
When you were plundered from me
I pistolled myself dead.'

'O, but my hair, Henry,
I'll cleanse the dear Head's stain,
Wipe all the ruin from it,
And make all sound again.'

89

So wise, so dear, her pleading,
I could not scorn her plea,
I willed myself to take her,
My darling-dear, to me . . .

But then, my wounds broke open,
From head and bosom broke
At once, the numbing blood-stream
And I awoke . . . I woke.